A Day to Remember

_____
Name

CHILD OF _____

WAS REBORN THROUGH WATER AND THE WORD
in

~ HOLY BAPTISM ~

ON _____
Date

AT _____
Name of Congregation

_____
City, State

BY _____
Name of Pastor

OTHER SPECIAL PEOPLE INVOLVED:

_____

_____

_____

The BAPTISM of Your Child

The BAPTISM of Your Child

THOMAS E. FAST AND CARLA H. FAST

CONCORDIA PUBLISHING HOUSE · SAINT LOUIS

1 2 3 4 5 6 7 8 9 10   16 15 14 13 12 11 10 09 08 07

CONTENTS

NOTES

NEW BIRTH

AS YOU WELCOME YOUR CHILD

Whether or not this is your first child, parenthood brings feelings of joy and wonder with each birth. However, along with excitement comes the responsibility of providing for another life—seeing to your baby's welfare physically, emotionally, and most important, spiritually. Scripture and our Lutheran Confessions call Baptism a second birth, the creation of a brand-new life begun in Christ, and reaching its fullness on the day of resurrection. By preparing to bring your child to be baptized you are taking the most important step in raising your child in the Christian faith.

In this book you will find information and help as you prepare for your child's Baptism, as well as for the formative years that follow. Whether you are a lifelong Lutheran or a new Christian, you will find useful information included in these brief pages, such as the Scripture's teaching about Baptism, a look at the Baptism service itself, and everyday activities you can do with your child to nurture him or her in the baptismal life. Through your teaching, your child will learn to live from the eternal significances and benefits of this Sacrament.

Now, let's begin with prayer.

PRAYER OF THE PARENTS

AT THE BAPTISM OF A CHILD

Heavenly Father, You once judged the wicked world with a flood but saved and preserved Noah and his family in the ark. You once drowned Pharaoh and his army but delivered Your people Israel and led them through the Red Sea. When Your Son, Jesus Christ, was baptized, You set apart the Jordan River and all water to be a flood that washes away all sins. Please look with favor upon (*name*), that, through Your Holy Spirit, he (she) may be blessed with true faith. Use this saving flood of Baptism to wash away the sin that he (she) has inherited from Adam, and separate him (her) from the number of unbelievers. Preserve him (her) dry and secure in the holy ark of Your Christian Church, and make him (her) fervent in spirit and joyful in hope as he (she) walks through the wilderness of this life trusting in Your flood of forgiveness. Make (*name*) worthy to attain eternal life and keep him (her) watchful for Your Son's return, when He will bring all believers to His eternal promised land. In Your holy name I pray. Amen.

What Is Baptism?

Go therefore and make disciples of all nations, baptizing them

in the name of the Father and of the Son and of the Holy Spirit.

Matthew 28:19

There are many questions that could be asked regarding this divine gift called Holy Baptism. Perhaps this is the first time in a long while that you've thought about it. How do you learn about Baptism and what it means? There's a wonderful little handbook that Martin Luther wrote for parents to use with their children. He called it his Small Catechism. You might have thought that the Small Catechism was a book to be set aside once you were confirmed; however, it was actually written to assist Christian parents. In fact, Luther had you in mind when he wrote the Small Catechism—just see how he titled this part:

THE SACRAMENT OF HOLY BAPTISM
As the head of the family should teach it in a simple way to his household

Notice that Luther says the head of the family should be teaching all of the members of the house about Baptism. That's a big indicator of how important Holy Baptism is in the life of a Christian. It's also an indication of the importance of your role as a parent. Christian parenting includes the nurturing of this faith born in Baptism. It is your vocation, that is, your God-given calling as a parent. God has called you not only to provide for this child but also to teach him or her about our heavenly Father and His love for us through His Son, Jesus. Most people learn the dos and don'ts of raising a child from their own parents. As Luther tells us, Christian parents are to learn how to be teachers of the faith through the direction of our heavenly Father. Central to that calling is the head of the house's use of the Word of God in the home.

The genius of Luther's treatment of Baptism in his Small Catechism is found in the four questions he asks. In fact, they are questions a child might ask regarding any gift that was given to him. These are Luther's four questions:

1. What is Baptism?—"What is it?"

2. What benefits does Baptism give?—"What does it do?"

3. How can water do such great things?—"How does it work?"

4. What does such baptizing with water indicate?—

"Why are you giving it to me?"

We'll see how Luther answers these introductory questions in the next section.

First
What is Baptism?

Baptism is not just plain water, but it is the water included in God's command and combined with God's word.

Which is that word of God?

Christ our Lord says in the last chapter of Matthew: "Therefore go and make disciples of all nations, baptizing them in the name of the Father and of the Son and of the Holy Spirit." **(Matt. 28:19)**

Luther's first question, "What is Baptism?" addresses the nature of Holy Baptism. Simply put, Holy Baptism is the application of water upon your child in the name of the Holy Trinity—the Father and the Son and the Holy Spirit. Plain water is used in this sacrament, it is true. But it is not plain water alone.

In Matthew 28:19, our Lord Jesus Christ, following His death and resurrection and just before His ascension, gives the Church the gift of Holy Baptism.

So it is that the water of Holy Baptism is used according to Jesus' command and combined with the name of God and all that name stands for. This God-given reality changes everything about this particular application of water. This leads us to the second question of Luther's Small Catechism.

Second
What benefits does Baptism give?

It works forgiveness of sins, rescues from death and the devil, and gives eternal salvation to all who believe this, as the words and promises of God declare.

Which are these words and promises of God?

Christ our Lord says in the last chapter of Mark: "Whoever believes and is baptized will be saved, but whoever does not believe will be condemned." **(Mark 16:16)**

Holy Baptism is a sacrament. A sacrament is "a sacred act instituted by God, in which God Himself has joined His Word of promise to a visible element, and by which He offers, gives, and seals the forgiveness of sins earned by Christ" (SC, Explanation, #236). That is to say, God has made a saving promise and has attached that promise to the act of baptizing with water (the visible element) in His name.

Jesus suffered, died, and rose again in order to save people from the eternal death brought about by sin. Through His saving actions, Christ purchased and won salvation for all. Baptism delivers and bestows the benefits of Jesus' redemption upon your child. Let's explore more deeply what those benefits mean for you and your child.

"It works forgiveness of sins."

(see Acts 2:38 and 22:16)

Everyone is conceived and born in sin (Psalm 51:5). Therefore, every child is, by nature, an object of wrath (Ephesians 2:3), that is, at enmity with God. This includes your child! There is no greater trouble your child faces than this. Yet it is right here where Baptism is such a great gift for him or her. In Baptism, the Lord tears down the barrier of sin that separates us from God. Baptism frees your child from the eternal consequences of sin. Jesus has taken upon Himself God's punishment for sin, and God reconciles Himself to us by crediting to us the forgiveness of sins won by Christ at Calvary's cross.

With the washing of Holy Baptism, your child is clean and holy and under the good favor of God. Baptism frees him or her to live forever as a "favorite" of the Lord, a beloved child of God. Through the forgiveness of sins, your son or daughter has the same place in the lap of the Father as does the only-begotten Son.

"Rescues from death and the devil"

(see Romans 6:3, 5; Galatians 3:27)

Imagine that you were living day after day on death row. What could you look forward to? Only death and the grave await you. This is all that awaits everyone who lives a life apart from Christ. They are living under a death sentence of sorts. God's wrath demands payment for sin. Those found guilty will be condemned to eternal death, that is, eternal separation from God. The Bible also calls this eternal separation "hell" and "damnation" and "the place reserved for the devil and his followers."

God teaches us in His Word that eternal death is the fair wage paid to us because of our sin (Romans 6:23). In other words, death is what we sinners deserve. What this means is that no matter how hard we work, how many ladders we climb, how many provisions we make for our children to be successful in life, or how great a success we seem to make of our lives, in the end it all comes to nothing. We eventually wind up not only in a grave, but eternally separated from God.

Enter Jesus. He takes our sins upon Himself. He takes our place on death row. He removes the power death has over us. In other words, He pays sin's wage for us and in a blessed exchange gives us resurrection and eternal life. In Baptism, Christ gives all of this to us so we no longer live under the sentence of death. Instead, we joyfully live, anticipating our resurrection and eternal life with Christ.

While we are no longer under the dominion of death, we still encounter it in all kinds of ways before the grave. Little deaths are all around us—for example, broken bones, broken homes, broken families, loss of loved ones, loss of health. These are all little foretastes of the grave that tug at you (and your children!). They are used by the devil to torment you along life's way and cause you to despair and doubt the mercy of God. Because being baptized means that death has no real hold on us, we don't need to despair over these little deaths. We can face these torments and encounters with the devil because of the promise that we have in Baptism—that through Holy Baptism, God rescues us from death and the devil.

"Gives eternal salvation"
(see Mark 16:16, Titus 3:5)

The children of Israel had been freed from over 400 years of harsh treatment and enslavement to Pharaoh and the Egyptians. Moses was leading them to the Promised Land, the land flowing with milk and honey. There they were, helpless with the Red Sea in front of them and Pharaoh and his armies hot on their trail. They seemed doomed. Yet when all appeared lost, the Lord parted the waters of the Red Sea. The people of Israel passed safely through the waters. Pharaoh's armies pursued, but were drowned by these waters. God's people were saved from their enemies.

Salvation is the merciful work of God to rescue the doomed and the helpless. Imagine if you had been an Israelite at the edge of the Red Sea. How terrifying would it have been to know you were being hunted down by an enemy who wants only your destruction? How utterly wonderful was the act of God to save you through the parting of the waters! Yet the salvation

God works through the water of Holy Baptism is greater than the salvation worked by the Lord at the Red Sea. Baptism is not a rescue from any man's army, but a rescue from the greatest enemies that can be faced—sin, death, and the devil. Baptism gifts your child with this greater salvation. True, this salvation will be unfolded fully only on the day of the resurrection of all flesh, but being baptized means it is a present possession, not only a future hope. What courage this gives both you and your child to face any and every enemy encountered—be it a Pharaoh or another—with the certain knowledge that almighty God has made eternal plans for each of His children.

Third

How can water do such great things?

Certainly not just water, but the word of God in and with the water does these things, along with the faith which trusts this word of God in the water. For without God's word the water is plain water and no Baptism. But with the word of God it is a Baptism, that is, a life-giving water, rich in grace, and a washing of the new birth in the Holy Spirit, as St. Paul says in Titus, chapter three:

"He saved us through the washing of rebirth and renewal by the Holy Spirit, whom He poured out on us generously through Jesus Christ our Savior, so that, having been justified by His grace, we might become heirs having the hope of eternal life. This is a trustworthy saying." **(Titus 3:5–8)**

"Works forgiveness of sins . . . rescues from death and the devil . . . gives eternal salvation." All of this from a little sprinkling of water and a few uttered words? Yes! It should be no surprise. The Lord has used water and His Word to accomplish great things on many occasions. Take, for example, the Old Testament story of the cleansing of Naaman (2 Kings 5:1–14).

Naaman was a commander of the army of Syria. When he found he had leprosy, he was desperate for a cure. A servant girl, an Israelite, encouraged her master to seek out the prophet Elisha for help. Elisha, speaking the Word of the Lord, commanded Naaman to wash seven times in the Jordan River. Along with the command to wash was the promise that he would be cleansed from his leprosy. Naaman rejected Elisha's direction. He was disgusted. He was expecting a spectacular cure from the prophet of God. Instead, all he got was common water combined with a few words. However, at the urging of his servants, he submitted himself to Elisha's directions. As a result, he was cured, and his skin "was restored like the flesh of a little child."

What gave the water of the Jordan River the power to cleanse Naaman? It was, after all, exactly what Naaman claimed: just plain water. But on that day, it was more—God attached His word and promise to the water, and that made it rich in grace. When God's word and promise are attached to the ordinary, it becomes extraordinary. The same is true of Baptism.

How can *water* do such great things? It is the Word of God combined with water that makes Baptism "quite a different thing from all other water . . . because something more noble is added here. God Himself stakes His honor, His power, and His might on it" (LC IV 17). Now when you look at the baptismal font filled with water, you can replace the common question, "Is that all there is?" with the certain promise, "There is all that!"

Fourth

*What does such baptizing
with water indicate?*

It indicates that the Old Adam in us should by daily contrition and repentance be drowned and die with all sins and evil desires, and that a new man should daily emerge and arise to live before God in righteousness and purity forever.

Where is this written?

St. Paul writes in Romans chapter six: "We were therefore buried with Him through baptism into death in order that, just as Christ was raised from the dead through the glory of the Father, we too may live a new life." **(Rom. 6:4)**

When your child is baptized, he or she is joined to the death and resurrection of Jesus Christ. The old Adam is put to death, and a new man, who lives by faith in Christ, is raised up. This death and resurrection sets the pattern and rhythm for the daily life of the baptized. It is the rhythm of daily repentance and faith. Daily, the baptized child of God, of every age, is to repent, that is, to turn away from sin. Daily, the baptized then turns to Christ and clings to Him in faith for the forgiveness of sins. This is the rhythm of the new life given in Holy Baptism. It is baptismal living. It is the life of the Christian.

Nurture this pattern of Christian living in your child. This is one of the most comforting aspects of being a Christian parent. You have the privilege of blessing your son or daughter with the comfort of forgiveness and absolution. As parents, you teach your child to live a life of repentance and faith. No longer is your child to deal with sin by clinging to it, justifying it, making excuses for it, or feeling guilty about it. Whereas the rest of the world tries to excuse sin, to hide it, to dismiss its seriousness, or to cover it up, Christians know how to truly deal with it. Teach your child not only to acknowledge sin but to confess it, to turn from it, and to cling to the forgiveness that God freely gives him or her through Christ. This is the pattern of living in repentance. This new life of faith is what "baptizing with water indicates."

HOLY BAPTISM

THE ORDER OF SERVICE

ORDER OF BAPTISM

Let's look at the baptismal rite commonly used in the Lutheran Church. The wording of the service of Holy Baptism is located on the left side of the page; a brief commentary is on the right. It is good to familiarize yourself with this rite, so you can understand what will happen and can ask your pastor about any sections that may not be clear to you.

An appropriate baptismal hymn may be sung. The candidate(s), sponsors, and family gather with the pastor at the entrance of the nave or at the font.

When candidates are unable to speak for themselves, the sponsors answer the questions on their behalf.

Stand

[P] In the name of the Father and of the ✝ Son and of the Holy Spirit.

Matthew 28:19b

[C] **Amen.**

THE INVOCATION

We call upon the triune God at the onset of worship to bless that which will follow and to confess the true God to whom we direct our worship. The trinitarian invocation also recalls our Baptism. We call on the Father, Son, and Holy Spirit, in whose name we are baptized. "For through Him we both have access in one Spirit to the Father" (Ephesians 2:18).

Here at the beginning of the rite, the use of the Invocation recognizes that the Baptism which will follow is done "in the name of," that is, by the authority of the Holy Trinity. The Baptism of your child is not the pastor's work; it is the Lord's work being done through the pastor.

P Dearly beloved, Christ our Lord says in the last chapter of Matthew, "All authority in heaven and on earth has been given to Me. Therefore go and make disciples of all nations, baptizing them in the name of the Father and of the Son and of the Holy Spirit." In the last chapter of Mark our Lord promises, "Whoever believes and is baptized will be saved." And the apostle Peter has written, "Baptism now saves you."

Matthew 28:18b–19; Mark 16:16a; 1 Peter 3:21

The Word of God also teaches that we are all conceived and born sinful and are under the power of the devil until Christ claims us as His own. We would be lost forever unless delivered from sin, death, and everlasting condemnation. But the Father of all mercy and grace has sent His Son Jesus Christ, who atoned for the sin of the whole world, that whoever believes in Him should not perish but have eternal life.

The pastor addresses each candidate:
P How are you named?
R *Name*

The pastor makes the sign of the holy cross upon the forehead and heart of each candidate while saying:
P *Name* , receive the sign of the holy cross both upon your ☩ forehead and upon your ☩ heart to mark you as one redeemed by Christ the crucified.

THE BAPTISMAL ADDRESS

This address presents the Scripture's account of the Lord's institution of Holy Baptism. It then proclaims Baptism's benefits: namely, your child will be made a disciple of the Lord and will receive the salvation Christ worked for him or her on the cross. This is your child's greatest need, for all are born sinful and separated from God. Here, in Baptism, Christ will claim your child as His own, so he or she will be delivered from sin, death, and eternal condemnation.

GIVING OF THE NAME

Your son or daughter's name is important. You spent a lot of time selecting the perfect name for your child. Perhaps you chose a family name, a biblical one, or one with a certain meaning. This Christian name, your child's first and middle names, will be used throughout the baptismal rite. This is significant, for God says to His children, "Fear not, for I have redeemed you; I have called you by name, you are Mine" (Isaiah 43:1).

GIVING OF THE SIGN OF THE CROSS

This is an ancient ceremony associated with Holy Baptism. It signifies that the benefits of Christ's cross are being given to your child through this sacrament. The sign of the cross becomes the possession of the baptized. As your

P Let us pray.
Almighty and eternal God,
according to Your strict judgment You condemned
    the unbelieving world through the flood,
yet according to Your great mercy You preserved
    believing Noah and his family,
    eight souls in all.
You drowned hard-hearted Pharaoh and all his host
    in the Red Sea,
yet led Your people Israel through the water on dry
    ground, foreshadowing this washing of Your
    Holy Baptism.
Through the Baptism in the Jordan of Your beloved
    Son, our Lord Jesus Christ,
You sanctified and instituted all waters to be a blessed
    flood and a lavish washing away of sin.

We pray that You would behold _name(s)_ according
    to Your boundless mercy
and bless _him/her/them_ with true faith by
    the Holy Spirit,
that through this saving flood all sin in _him/her/them_ ,
    which has been inherited from Adam
    and which _he himself / she herself / they themselves
    has/have_ committed since,
would be drowned and die.
Grant that _he/she/they_ be kept safe and secure in the
    holy ark of the Christian Church,
    being separated from the multitude of unbelievers
    and serving Your name at all times with a fervent
    spirit and a joyful hope,
so that, with all believers in Your promise,
    he/she/they would be declared worthy
    of eternal life;
through Jesus Christ, our Lord. (501)
C **Amen.**

child matures, he or she may wish to make the sign of the cross by tracing it upon the body. With that body language, your child is confessing the baptismal faith and remembering the blessings received in the sacrament. Baptized children often make the sign of the cross before prayer when rising in the morning, when going to sleep at night, and in times of trouble. Another appropriate time to use the sign is whenever the pastor blesses the baptized.

PRAYER

This prayer is taken from Martin Luther's baptismal rite and has commonly been called the "Flood Prayer." It recounts baptismal imagery from the Old Testament and our Lord's own baptism. Wonderful in their own rights, the Old Testament accounts also foreshadow the greater saving flood that your child will encounter in Holy Baptism. These waters will wash away all sin that is inherited and every sin that is committed. Your child will be placed, safe and secure, in the ark of the Christian Church. This prayer petitions the Lord to make your son or daughter's Baptism a saving act, in accordance with His promise.

If the sponsors were previously enrolled, the service continues below with the Holy Gospel.

P From ancient times the Church has observed the custom of appointing sponsors for baptismal candidates and catechumens. In the Evangelical Lutheran Church sponsors are to confess the faith expressed in the Apostles' Creed and taught in the Small Catechism. They are, whenever possible, to witness the Baptism of those they sponsor. They are to pray for them, support them in their ongoing instruction and nurture in the Christian faith, and encourage them toward the faithful reception of the Lord's Supper. They are at all times to be examples to them of the holy life of faith in Christ and love for the neighbor.

The pastor addresses the sponsors.

P Is it your intention to serve __name of candidate(s)__ as sponsors in the Christian faith?

R *Yes, with the help of God.*

P God enable you both to will and to do this faithful and loving work and with His grace fulfill what we are unable to do.

C **Amen.**

P Hear the Holy Gospel according to St. Mark.

They brought young children to [Jesus] that He might touch them; but the disciples rebuked those who brought them. But when Jesus saw it, He was greatly displeased and said to them, "Let the little children come to Me, and do not forbid them; for of such is the kingdom of God. Assuredly, I say to you, whoever does not receive the kingdom of God as a little child will by no means enter it." And He took them up in His arms, put His hands on them, and blessed them.

Mark 10:13–16 NKJV

P This is the Word of the Lord.

C **Thanks be to God.**

ADDRESS TO SPONSORS

In Baptism, your child will be made a part of a new family—the Holy Christian Church. This means the members of the Church are now your child's siblings. Because your child's brothers and sisters have an interest in their new sibling, sponsors are usually assigned to your child. These sponsors are representatives of the Church and are asked to support and encourage the parents in the ongoing nurture of the baptized child. If necessary, the sponsors act as parental substitutes attending to the faith of the baptized, should the child lose his or her parents. For this reason, the selection of sponsors should be made with great care. It is most fitting for the sponsors to be selected from among the faithful of the congregation. At the least, the sponsors should believe and confess the faith into which the child is baptized. In this section, the sponsors state their intention to serve the baptized in this way.

GOSPEL READING

This Gospel reading is St. Mark's account of Jesus' blessing the little children. Jesus says that whoever does not receive the kingdom as a little child will by no means enter it. A little child earns nothing. Whatever he or she has is a gift; nothing is gained for himself. Young or old, everyone receives the kingdom in the same way—as a little child— only as a gift. So it is with the blessings that Baptism brings. Baptism is all God's work, not the work of the baptized. It is pure gift. This Gospel is read to emphasize the gifting nature of Baptism.

The pastor places his hands on the head(s) of the candidate(s), and the congregation joins in praying:

C   **Our Father who art in heaven,**
      hallowed be Thy name,
      Thy kingdom come,
      Thy will be done on earth as it is
        in heaven;
      give us this day our daily bread;
      and forgive us our trespasses as we
        forgive those who trespass against us;
      and lead us not into temptation,
      but deliver us from evil.

Matthew 6:9–13

  For Thine is the kingdom and the power and the glory forever and ever. Amen.

If the baptismal party has stood at the entrance of the nave to this point, they now move to the font. A hymn may be sung during the procession. Then the pastor says:

P   The Lord preserve your coming in and your going out from this time forth
and even ✠ forevermore.

C   **Amen.**

Sit

The pastor addresses the candidate(s) and asks the following questions:

P   <u> Name(s) </u>, do you renounce the devil?

R   *Yes, I renounce him.*

P   Do you renounce all his works?

R   *Yes, I renounce them.*

P   Do you renounce all his ways?

R   *Yes, I renounce them.*

P   Do you believe in God, the Father Almighty, maker of heaven and earth?

R   *Yes, I believe.*

continued on next page

THE LORD'S PRAYER

When faith speaks, it prays. Jesus gave us the Lord's Prayer in response to His disciples' plea of "teach us how to pray." It is the family prayer of the Christian Church. In Holy Baptism, your child is made a child of God. Now he or she is privileged to call God "Father." In fact, the Small Catechism reminds us that the words "Our Father who art in heaven" mean that "God tenderly invites us to believe that He is our true Father and that we are His true children, so that with all boldness and confidence we may ask Him as dear children ask their dear father."

RENUNCIATION OF THE DEVIL/CONFESSION OF THE APOSTLES' CREED

The faith into which your child is being baptized is confessed in the Apostles' Creed. The devil, the enemy of God, is renounced, as is his lordship over the life of the baptized. Your child is being brought under new ownership in Baptism—that of the Holy Trinity. If your child is too young to articulate the faith, you, as parents, along with the sponsors and/or congregation will speak in his or her stead. This is the confession in which you are called as parents to raise your child.

continued from previous page

P Do you believe in Jesus Christ, His only Son, our Lord, who was conceived by the Holy Spirit, born of the virgin Mary, suffered under Pontius Pilate, was crucified, died and was buried; He descended into hell; the third day He rose again from the dead; He ascended into heaven and sits at the right hand of God the Father Almighty; from thence He will come to judge the living and the dead?

R *Yes, I believe.*

P Do you believe in the Holy Spirit, the holy Christian Church, the communion of saints, the forgiveness of sins, the resurrection of the body, and the life everlasting?

R *Yes, I believe.*

P   *Name*, do you desire to be baptized?

R *Yes, I do.*

The pastor pours water three times on the head of each candidate while saying:

P   *Name*, I baptize you in the name of the Father and of the Son and of the Holy Spirit.

C **Amen.**

The pastor places his hands on the head of the newly baptized while saying:

P The almighty God and Father of our Lord Jesus Christ, who has given you the new birth of water and of the Spirit and has forgiven you all your sins, strengthen you with His grace to life ☩ everlasting.

C **Amen.**

The pastor may place a white garment on the newly baptized while saying:

P Receive this white garment to show that you have been clothed with the robe of Christ's righteousness that covers all your sin. So shall you stand without fear before the judgment seat of Christ to receive the inheritance prepared for you from the foundation of the world.

THE BAPTISM

With the application of the water and the invoking of the Name comes the actual Baptism. Here your son or daughter receives the new birth and all the blessings the Lord has promised to attach to this washing.

WHITE GARMENT

In Baptism, your child has "put on Christ" (Galatians 3:27); that is, he or she has been covered with the righteousness of Christ. Your child is now a co-heir with Christ of His glory. A white garment may be given to signify this reality.

The pastor may light a baptismal candle from the paschal candle and give it to the newly baptized while saying:

P Receive this burning light to show that you have received Christ who is the Light of the world. Live always in the light of Christ, and be ever watchful for His coming, that you may meet Him with joy and enter with Him into the marriage feast of the Lamb in His kingdom, which shall have no end.

CANDLE

A candle may be lit from the paschal candle and given as a sign of the share that your child has now been given in Christ's victory over death. Light not only signifies the glory of Christ (2 Corinthians 4:6) but also the reality that each Christian is called to be prepared to meet Him on the Last Day (Matthew 25:1–13). This candle can now be used during family devotions, or it can be lit during the celebration of future baptismal birthdays.

The newly baptized may be welcomed with the following:

A In Holy Baptism God the Father has made you _a member / members_ of His Son, our Lord Jesus Christ, and _an heir / heirs_ with us of all the treasures of heaven in the one holy Christian and apostolic Church. We receive you in Jesus' name as our _brother(s)/sister(s)_ in Christ, that together we might hear His Word, receive His gifts, and proclaim the praises of Him who called us out of darkness into His marvelous light.

C **Amen. We welcome you in the name of the Lord.**

WELCOME

In Baptism, your child has become a child of God and a member of God's family. As fellow-members of that family, the congregation welcomes your child as the newest of its members.

26

Stand

P Let us pray.
    Almighty and most merciful God and Father, we thank and praise You that You graciously preserve and enlarge Your family and have granted _name(s)_ the new birth in Holy Baptism and made _him/her/them_ _a member / members_ of Your Son, our Lord Jesus Christ, and _an heir / heirs_ of Your heavenly kingdom. We humbly implore You that, as _he/she/they_ _has/have_ now become Your _child/children_, You would keep _him/her/them_ in _his/her/their_ baptismal grace, that according to Your good pleasure _he/she/they_ may faithfully grow to lead a godly life to the praise and honor of Your holy name and finally, with all Your saints, obtain the promised inheritance in heaven; through Jesus Christ, our Lord. (503)

C **Amen.**

P Peace ✝ be with you.
C **Amen.**

All return to their places.

PRAYER

A final prayer is offered for the newly baptized, that your child might be kept living in his or her Baptism unto life everlasting.

Now that your child has been baptized, you are parents of a newborn all over again! The new life of faith born in your child needs to be nurtured and strengthened. Your calling as parents is to tend to this. You are to see that the Word of God, through instruction and attendance in the Divine Service, feeds your child's faith. The following section of this book will explain your role in more detail and will offer suggestions to aid you in this blessed responsibility.

NOTES

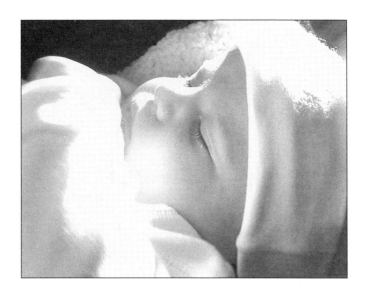

GIVEN BY GOD

. . . teaching them to observe all that I have commanded you.

Matthew 28:20

Jesus came and said to them, "All authority in heaven and on earth has been given to me. Go therefore and make disciples of all nations, baptizing them in the name of the Father and of the Son and of the Holy Spirit, teaching them to observe all that I have commanded you. And behold, I am with you always, to the end of the age." Matthew 28:18–20

When our Lord instituted Baptism, He intended Baptism and the teaching of the faith to go hand in hand. These two activities are not to be separated because one does not come without the other. Just as God has called you to be parents through the gift of your child, you are called to raise him or her in the true faith. This means that the responsibility of teaching your child the Christian faith belongs to you.

This activity of using the Word of God to instruct and nurture the faith born in Baptism has a churchly name—"catechesis." Catechesis is mandatory because it is nourishment. As with any birth, nourishment is necessary to continue life. The child of God born of water and the Word needs ongoing spiritual nourishment. Your child needs that which will strengthen the life of faith born in Baptism—the very Word of God. Without regular instruction, without this spiritual food, the gift of faith will be undeveloped, it will be weak, and it could even die. Baptism cannot be undone—but the new life given in Baptism can be killed.

Consider the words and admonition of Luther:

Remember, therefore, that it is no joke to take sides against the devil and not only to drive him away from the little child, but to burden the child with such a mighty and lifelong enemy. Remember, too, that it is very necessary to aid the poor child with all your heart and strong faith, earnestly to intercede for him that God, in accordance with this prayer, would not only free him from the power of the devil, but also strengthen him, so that he may nobly resist the devil in life and in death. And I suspect that people turn out so badly after baptism because our concern for them has been so cold and careless; we, at their baptism, interceded for them without zeal.

While this responsibility is daunting, the Lord does not leave you to accomplish it alone. He will use His Holy Spirit to strengthen you for the task, and He places you and your baptized child into the fellowship of the Church. This fellowship, and your role within it, is discussed in the next section.

THE RESPONSIBILITY OF THE PARENTS

Your newly baptized child is now a member of a much larger family—the family of God. An old folk proverb declares that it takes a village to raise a child. From a Christian standpoint, we can say that it takes the family of God to raise a child. This raising occurs through regular attendance at the Divine Service. Here is where your child meets his heavenly Father and hears his Father's voice as the Word of God is read and preached and administered in the Sacraments. Here is where the child of God will be surrounded by the life-nurturing words of his Father as they circulate among the family of God in hymnody, prayer, and creed. Here is also where you will receive support and encouragement as you fulfill your parental duties toward your child. Although pastors, teachers, family, and friends can help, the primary responsibilities of raising a child in the faith ultimately lie with you. Regular attendance at the Divine Service will strengthen you.

And what are those responsibilities? To provide a loving home for the children entrusted to their care. Under the umbrella of "a loving home" is the nurture of the Christian faith. The head of the house is responsible for the spiritual, as well as physical, feeding of the family. This is not just helpful advice; rather, it is a command from God Himself. "Fathers, do not provoke your children to anger, but bring them up in the discipline and instruction of the Lord" (Ephesians 6:4). God does not want the faith of His little ones to wither; therefore, parents must take their responsibilities seriously.

Statistics show that the average 21-year-old has fallen away from the Church, from Baptism, and therefore from God. Many attempts have been made to address the problem. Sunday Schools, Lutheran Day Schools, youth groups, specially trained practitioners and Directors of Christian Education—all are designed to keep children active within the family of God. But what's missing from the picture? That's right—active, committed parents! Parents are those called by God to nurture and catechize their children. While others may assist you in this task, it is primarily yours. Therefore, it is of utmost importance that you as parents provide sound catechesis. All parents teach, even "bad" parents. Those who abandon their responsibility to catechize are still teaching their children—teaching them to find their life and worth in something other than the Word of God. If the Christian faith is not nurtured with the Word of God by the parents, something else takes its place.

Claim this God-given responsibility as your own. It is through you that God will bless His new child, nurturing his or her faith unto life everlasting.

The following portion of the book contains ideas you might find useful as your family develops its devotional life, centered upon the Word of God, and the life given to us in that Word.

The First Year

IN THE BEGINNING

Just as a house must have a good foundation to support the structure on top of it, a Christian must have a firm foundation. As a result of Holy Baptism, your child has Christ as the foundation upon which to build his or her life. The following section contains little building blocks to assist you as you bring your child up in the Christian faith.

 Home Life

Prior to your child's birth, you began planning for a homecoming. How long did it take you to decorate the nursery? You probably spent some time selecting a theme, buying coordinating items, painting the walls the perfect colors, and adding special touches here and there. What about reminders of your baby's Baptism and new life in Christ? Celebrate this new life—give it a place of honor in your home.

Photo (large) © istockphoto.com/Adriane Dworzak
Photo (small) © istockphoto.com/Franklin Lugenbeel

Consider the following additions to the nursery:

- A baptismal certificate or banner. Many parents frame a certificate and hang it on the wall of their children's bedroom. Such certificates indicate the Baptism dates of the children. Many are made of paper; some are stitched in embroidery. Banners are also lovely reminders of your child's new birth.

- A picture or portrait of Christ. Along with family pictures, one of Christ is often placed in the bedroom. There are many such pictures available; children respond to ones that are lifelike, as opposed to cartoon characters.

- A crucifix. Place a crucifix above the bed of each child. It serves as a reminder of Christ's sacrificial death and resurrection for each of us. Some people prefer the use of a cross with a small shell attached at the center point. The shell represents Baptism and reminds the child that he or she is a member of God's family.

- Noah's ark items. What about all of the Noah's ark merchandise available for nurseries and children's rooms? It is a very popular theme, with lots of sweet images. But the account of Noah isn't sweet—it's about death and life. Noah is about Baptism! God brought forth new life from the floodwaters.

- A baptismal mobile. Create a mobile using felt cut into symbols of the faith. Include a cross, shell, chalice, wafer, or other items signifying God's mercy toward His children.

The baby's room is not the entire home; take a new look at your surroundings. Are there other places where cues of God's love and mercy can be placed?

- Crosses are symbols of Jesus' sacrifice for mankind.

- Favorite Scripture verses in calligraphy or embroidery serve to keep the Word of God foremost in our thoughts. Fill your home with reminders of God's love and mercy.

- Perhaps the obvious place is the bathroom. Water and the Word—daily washing away of the dirt and grime of life serve as a reminder of the washing received in Holy Baptism.

All of these ideas serve as reminders for your family. They communicate the message of God's love and forgiveness to those in your home. Communication is very important, not only in our lives, but in those of young children.

We know that babies are capable of learning many things. The beginning stages of life outside the womb are ones filled with constant learning and growing. In fact, your child was doing these things prior to birth. Recall the account of the Virgin Mary's visit to her cousin, Elizabeth. John, the baby in Elizabeth's womb, leaped at the recognition of the child Mary was carrying (Luke 1). John was definitely alive and kicking! And like other babies, he listened to his mother speak and sing to him.

- Talk to your child about God. Have conversations as you dress your newest family member, change diapers, eat, and otherwise spend your day. Relate the wonders of the world that God has given to us. Speak about the mercy of Christ, His death and resurrection. In other words, include discussions about Jesus in your everyday "conversations" with your baby.

- Sing hymns and songs of Baptism in your daily serenades. There are many hymns that you can learn by heart. Use Baptism hymns during bath time, Advent hymns during the Advent Season, etc. (See p. 62–63 for a list of songs to memorize.)

- As you relate to the other members of your house, speak the language of the Church. Talk of Baptism, God's love for your family, His daily caring for the family at Church, etc. As your little one matures, he or she will understand these concepts as they relate to everyday circumstances, already being familiar with the repetition of the words.

Talking about God and His love for us is important, but it is not a substitute for hearing about it from God Himself. The Divine Service is the "real thing." It is where God comes to us with His gifts of life and salvation—not just talking about them, but delivering them to you and your family.

 Church Life

Baptism is the beginning of the Christian's life in Christ. Once life is given, it needs to be fed. You certainly wouldn't deny your baby nourishment for his or her body; neither should you for his or her soul.

- The Divine Service is where God comes to us with His gifts of life and salvation—for you and for your baby. Set the groundwork now for weekly attendance. As your child grows, the knowledge that Sunday is the Lord's Day will be the highest priority.

- Where to sit? In the back? Up front? It's truly up to you, but please understand most people are not offended or upset if babies cry or fuss during the service. Some churches have even replaced the back row of pews with rocking chairs in order to allow parents to remain in the service while calming a fussy little one.

- Note the sections of the liturgy that you know by heart. Make a plan to use these sections in your daily singing. As your child grows, he or she will already know part of the liturgy and will be able to participate with the rest of the family during the Divine Service.

 Rituals/Traditions

Attendance at the Divine Service is an important part of your family's life. So, too, is the life within your home. Consider your family rituals. Every family has them, from the special way you say good morning to the repeated readings of a favorite book. Remember, kids love to do the same thing night after night. If you forget to read that special story, someone will tell you about it! Begin some family rituals that you can use to share God's love with your family.

GIVEN BY GOD

- Start and end each day with prayer. Pray for your child. Thank God for the gift of your family and for making all of you members of His family. If you have not already done so, begin having family devotions. Include the Ten Commandments, the Apostles' Creed, and the Lord's Prayer. See the section on the family altar for home devotion ideas; also note the list of hymns to sing to/with your child.

- Sing hymns each day. Repeat hymns often—perhaps as a hymn of the month. You'll be surprised to find that when your child is older, he or she will probably know the words to some hymns by heart, just from listening to you over time.

- As you tell your baby and the other members of your family that you love them, remind them of God's love. Tell them that you're thankful that God has made you a family. When you tell each other good night, tell them to sleep soundly in Jesus' love.

NOTES

The Second Year

REPETITION . . . REPETITION . . . REPETITION

Many changes accompany the first year of life. As your baby begins the second year, growth continues in astounding ways. Your child knows you and the other members of the family. The "world" is your home, with you, the parents, who are to nurture and shape the lives God has entrusted to you. Add to the building blocks that you used during the first year of life.

Home Life

You're listening for the sounds of words coming forth. By now you recognize what various cries or gurgles mean. Your child is communicating with you in many ways. This development will continue to manifest itself in the utterance of sounds and words.

- Talk to your child. Just as you continue to tell your baby the same things repeatedly (I love you, Mamma, Daddy), use faith language. Use vocabulary from the liturgy, from Scripture, from hymnody. Include words such as God, Jesus, forgiveness, Baptism, faith, etc. While your baby will not understand all that is said, language development continues at a rapid rate. Repetition is important.

- Sing hymns to your child. Music can be a source of comfort for young children. An added bonus is that your child will recognize these hymns when they are sung in church. In fact, many of the words will already be learned by heart.

- Use recordings of hymnody in your daily routines. Such music can be comforting during naptime. See pp. 62–63 for a list of hymns and songs to introduce to your child.

- Throughout the day, or at certain periods (such as before bedtime), read a story to your child. Do you remember your parents reading to you? Hopefully you had such heartwarming experiences. Now is the time for you to do so with your own little one. Short stories telling God's love for us as found in Scripture are available in a variety of reading materials. This is time spent hearing the Word of God, being with Mom and/or Dad, and growing in faith through such nurturing.

 Rituals/Traditions

Bath time is such a loving time between parents and their children. The warm water, combined with a gentle touch, allow a child to relax and, oftentimes, giggle with delight. As a result, children usually look forward to bath time as a special part of the day. What a wonderful, appropriate setting to talk of Baptism. Talk about washing sins away. Say the words of the Invocation. Use a special washcloth (name embroidered) to bathe. Remember Baptism and celebrate it—you *are* baptized, not *were* baptized. Really, anytime water is used, you can relate it to Baptism.

- Another time to remind your child of Baptism is in the morning. While dressing your child, remind him or her that those who were baptized have put on Christ.

- Don't forget about your morning and evening routines. Begin and end your day in the name of the Lord. Make the sign of the cross over your child when he or she awakens, and again at bedtime. This is done in remembrance of Baptism. It is a reminder that your child belongs to God. He or she is a child of the heavenly Father with all of the benefits that name brings.

- Continue your prayer and devotional time. Pray for your child. Remember his or her Baptism; rejoice that your child is a child of the heavenly Father. Begin teaching the foundations of the faith—the Ten Commandments, the Apostles' Creed, and the Lord's Prayer. Say and pray them daily, and your son or daughter will learn them by heart, without even realizing it and without trying to commit them to memory. These are important foundational building blocks of the Christian faith and life.

Church Life

Attendance at the Divine Service should be the highest priority. Sadly, many people get so involved in other aspects of their lives that church takes a backseat (or is completely kicked out of the car!) to other things. That is why it's important for you to schedule not only your family devotion time but also your time at church.

- Everything you do in your home devotions is in preparation for the Divine Service each week. All of the singing, praying, and reading point to the Divine Service, where God brings His gifts of life and salvation to you and your child. Go there as often as possible. Expose your child to the sights, sounds, movements, and smells of the Father's house. Instill the notion that this is where the family is to be on Sunday mornings.

- If you haven't considered it, think about moving toward the front of the sanctuary. Little ones can derive a lot from the goings-on during the Divine Service. By sitting at the front now, you are establishing the tradition that this is where the family goes to receive God's gifts.

NOTES

The Third Year

HERE WE GO!

On the move is a good way to describe your toddler. Everything is new, and there are many things to see and touch. With this in mind, provide opportunities for your child to "see and do" things in God's world.

Home Life

- Confession and absolution are important. Teach your toddler to confess sin at a young age; you, in turn, pronounce forgiveness for the sin. Develop this practice early so as to avoid the typical response to a sin—"Oh, that's okay." Sin is never okay; but we are okay because we are forgiven in Christ. The use of the forgiveness of sins is a good way to keep the Gospel at the center of family life.

- The Word of God—for you! Relate simple Bible stories, in book form and as storytelling. Toddlers love to hear the same stories repeatedly. Explain them in a simple way, telling your child that all of God's work is for him or her. After you read/tell the story, ask your child to tell it back to you.

- The world of words is opening up for your child. Record favorite stories or hymns for him or her to listen to during quiet time. The familiarity of your voice will soothe and comfort your child, just as the voice of our heavenly Father comforts us.

- As you go for strolls with your child, notice God's world around you. Talk about animals and birds, all of God's creation, and explain how it was made for us to take care of. A child's natural curiosity will lead to many questions for you. If you're not sure how to respond, just say so. Parents don't have to know all of the answers!

Church Life

- Continue your established pattern of attending the Divine Service. Arrive prior to the beginning of the service and take a tour of the sanctuary. Note the stained glass windows and the symbols located throughout the sanctuary. Explain the symbols to your child: shells representing Baptism, chalice and wafer symbolizing the Holy Supper. Don't try to find everything in one day—spread this out over several weeks.

- Make simple shapes that represent the various symbols found in your church. The shapes can be made from felt and placed in an easily made flannel book. Bring the book to church and match the shapes with their counterparts. Talk about what the symbols mean.

- Several of the church decorations change color with the seasons of the Church Year. Learn the various colors used for each season. As your child begins to notice, you can teach about the seasons and what they teach us. For example, during the Sundays after Pentecost your catechesis might include that the pretty green colors stand for growth and life. When you're outside, you can again note the green colors in the grass and leaves, also signs of growth and life.

- Toddlers want to be like Mommy and Daddy. Teach your child parts of the liturgy. Simple lines can be sung by all members of the family. Tell your child when to stand and sit in the service. Demonstrate how to fold hands during prayer and how to make the sign of the cross during the Invocation and at various times throughout the service.

- Many churches have Sunday School classes for children as young as two. Often these classes involve one or both parents as well as the children. Check with your pastor or Sunday School superintendent to see if classes are available at your congregation.

 Rituals/Traditions

By now you probably have several rituals in place. Those that involve simple ways of sharing God's love with your child could last a lifetime. For instance, instead of just celebrating your child's birthday, add a special celebration for his or her baptismal birthday. Make a cake in the shape of a cross. Sing baptismal songs, perhaps the ones sung at the Baptism itself.

As you continue with your family catechesis, be sure to include hymns that you have been singing to your child. Your youngest family members will enjoy participating in the devotional time by accompanying you during the singing.

- Mealtimes can be a great place for traditions. Teach your child simple prayers in thanksgiving for the many blessings God has given you. See p. 56 for such prayers.

- Little games can quickly become rituals. For instance, each morning as your child is learning to dress himself or herself, ask what is happening. The answer could be something such as, "I'm putting on Christ. I am a baptized child of God, ready to start my day!" Such snippets can quickly become favorite rituals for a toddler.

- Bedtime rituals can include a bath (baptismal reminder!), followed by a Bible story. After the story, it's time for prayers and sleep. Remind your children that they are in God's hands, and that He is watching over the entire family each night.

NOTES

The Rest of Childhood

Before you know it, your child will be past the toddler stage and embarking upon a childhood filled with school and friends, homework and social activities. Your home and church life will serve as anchors during these years. The spiritual nourishment that you provide for your child will enable him or her to continue to grow in Christ. Spend time with your child, teaching the faith and modeling it in your family. It is time you will never regret.

 Home Life

• As your child learns to read, make an alphabet list of scriptural words to correspond with each letter. Post these words on pages that can be hung in the bedroom or placed into a folder for a keepsake.

• Promote your child's understanding of the written word by labeling items throughout the house. Use index cards to label things such as "Bible," "cross," "candle."

- Provide a wealth of reading material, using Bible story books appropriate for the age level of your child(ren). Read with your child; tape stories for assisted reading; allow time for independent study.

- Playtime can also be used as a reminder of God's love. Children often use dolls or action figures to act out stories or other scenarios. Encourage the use of Bible accounts during such times.

- Continue to provide recordings of hymnody for use during quiet or nap times. Such music can also be used during study time as your child matures.

- There are a variety of arts and crafts activities available to accompany Bible stories. Such projects usually involve creating a keepsake to serve as a reminder of the story. These items can make nice gifts for your child to give to a friend or shut-in.

 ## Church Life

By now, your child knows that Sunday is the Lord's Day. Continue taking him or her to the Father's house weekly. Encourage participation in the Divine Service. Purchase a hymnal for your child—have it engraved if you can. Encourage your child to bring the hymnal to church and to use it often at home. When he or she is younger, just picking up the hymnal and opening it will suffice. Demonstrate how to find the services and hymns within the book. Over time, your child will be able to follow the Divine Service.

Another book for your child's collection is the Small Catechism. There is a copy of the catechism located within *Lutheran Service Book*. Some people prefer to have an independent copy of the catechism for note taking. Either way, the catechism should be on your child's "must have" book list.

If your church has a Day School, consider enrolling your child. A Christ-centered education can assist you in your catechesis of your child, and the benefits of such an education can be quite significant.

As your youngster grows, discuss the idea of vocation. Your child is a student, a friend, perhaps a sibling, a son or daughter, a child of God. Model the life of a servant, showing how God gives to us and how we, in turn, give to our neighbor. Encourage visiting the sick and shut-in, helping with various charity organizations, and donating funds to worthwhile causes.

 ### Rituals/Traditions

Continue the rituals and traditions that you have established. Add more if you wish. As your child grows, traditions become dearer because so much in your child's world is changing. Remind him or her that God's love for His children never changes.

Don't forget to pray with and for your child. Parenthood brings many responsibilities. Take your cares and concerns to the One who can handle every situation.

Practice Confession and Absolution in the home—remember, it's a daily living out of our Baptism! As your child matures, teach him or her to say what commandment has been broken, then pronounce forgiveness for the sin. Talk with your pastor about Private Confession and Absolution at church. Set aside times for the family to take advantage of this marvelous gift.

While your child is still young, start a family thanksgiving book. Each year, perhaps at the beginning of a new Church Year, have each member jot down a few things from the previous year that he or she is thankful for. In time, you will have a family treasury to be shared and enjoyed for generations to come.

Above all, remember to continue your family altar time. Switch times to fit busy schedules, just make sure you keep doing it. Most families have trouble eating one meal together; it's up to you to keep your family centered around the Word of God. It's a wonderful privilege to study God's Word. It's not something that we have to do—we get to do it. See the next section for information about the family altar.

NOTES

THE FAMILY ALTAR

Oh, blest the house, whate'er befall,

Where Jesus Christ is all in all!

LSB 862:1

Have you ever heard of a family altar? It's simply a space set apart in your home where your family gathers together to have devotions. Just as we have special places for eating, sleeping, and recreating, it is fitting that we also have a space set apart for prayer. This area can help prepare the members of the family for Word and prayer. It serves as a place to gather together (without distractions) for Scripture, prayer, and hymnody. Its presence in the home captures the attention, reminding the family that we gather together as a family of God to hear His Word and pray to Him.

Although the altar can be located anywhere within the home, select a prominent area with easy access for family members. A typical location is the dining room. In our home, we clear off the supper dishes and replace them with the altar items. We use the dining room because there is a chair for each person, and most are already in their seats! When our son was younger, however, we had the altar area in his bedroom because that was where he spent a lot of time. Wherever you decide to place your family altar, make sure there is enough room for all to gather and that the location is such to remind people of its presence.

Once you've determined where to place the altar area, it's time to decide what you should include in it. Think about what's on the altar in your church. Candles, a crucifix, a Bible—these items should be the focal point of your altar. Also include a hymnal (one copy for each reader in the family) and a catechism. That's it! If you want to add more, feel free to do so, but basically, you're set.

So, how do you use this altar? First, decide when the devotional time will take place. Set this time apart—no phone calls, no television, no interruption. Our family knows that Word and prayer occur immediately following supper. Thus it is understood that usually at 6:30 everyone is to be found gathered around the altar.

We've found that it helps to hook the altar time onto another regularly scheduled family activity. While ours comes at the end of supper, other families have devotions at 7:30 each morning. All children meet in the living room, with schoolbags in tow. Upon completion, everyone heads to school or work for the day. The time of day is not important; it's the scheduling of time for family catechesis that is—and scheduling is a way to make sure you'll do it. Our days are so filled with commitments that we must reserve this time for the benefit of our family or it will be overtaken by the press of the day and it will not get done.

What do you do at the family altar? You're building upon your daily prayer of the Ten Commandments, the Apostles' Creed, and the Lord's Prayer. Typically Scripture readings and hymn singing and other prayers are included. A format, similar to following the Divine Service in the hymnal, is used. For your convenience, orders for Morning and Evening Prayer are included on the following pages. As you follow the orders, include hymns and prayers as you find useful.

MORNING

The sign of the cross ✛ may be made by all in remembrance of their Baptism.

In the name of the Father and of the ✛ Son and of the Holy Spirit.
Amen.

In the morning, O Lord, You hear my voice;
in the morning I prepare a sacrifice for You and watch.   *Psalm 5:3*

My mouth is filled with Your praise,
and with Your glory all the day.   *Psalm 71:8*

O Lord, open my lips,
and my mouth will declare Your praise.   *Psalm 51:15*

Glory be to the Father and to the Son and to the Holy Spirit;
as it was in the beginning, is now, and will be forever. Amen.

A hymn, canticle, or psalm may be sung or spoken.

An appointed reading or one of the following is read: Colossians 3:1–4; Exodus 15:1–11; Isaiah 12:1–6; Matthew 20:1–16; Mark 13:32–36; Luke 24:1–9; John 21:4–14; Ephesians 4:17–24; Romans 6:1–4.

A portion of the Small or Large Catechism may be read.

The Apostles' Creed is confessed.

Lord's Prayer

Prayers for others and ourselves

Concluding prayers:
Almighty God, merciful Father, who created and completed all things, on this day when the work of our calling begins anew, we implore You to create its beginning, direct its continuance, and bless its end, that our doings may be preserved from sin, our life sanctified, and our work this day be well pleasing to You; through Jesus Christ, our Lord. (441)
Amen.

I thank You, my heavenly Father, through Jesus Christ, Your dear Son, that You have kept me this night from all harm and danger; and I pray that You would keep me this day also from sin and every evil, that all my doings and life may please You. For into Your hands I commend myself, my body and soul, and all things. Let Your holy angel be with me, that the evil foe may have no power over me. Amen. (423)
Small Catechism

Let us bless the Lord.   *[Psalm 103:1]*
Thanks be to God.

Then go joyfully to your work.

EARLY EVENING

The sign of the cross ☩ may be made by all in remembrance of their Baptism.

In the name of the Father and of the ☩ Son and of the Holy Spirit.
Amen.

A candle may be lighted.

Let my prayer rise before You as incense,
the lifting up of my hands as the evening sacrifice.   *Psalm 141:2*

Joyous light of glory:
of the immortal Father;
heavenly, holy, blessed Jesus Christ.
We have come to the setting of the sun,
and we look to the evening light.
We sing to God, the Father, Son, and Holy Spirit:
You are worthy of being praised with pure voices forever.
O Son of God, O Giver of life: the universe proclaims Your glory.

A hymn, canticle, or psalm may be sung or spoken.

An appointed reading or one of the following is read: Luke 24:28–31; Exodus 16:11–21, 31; Isaiah 25:6–9; Matthew 14:15–21; Matthew 27:57–60; Luke 14:15–24; John 6:25–35; John 10:7–18; Ephesians 6:10–18a.

A portion of the Small or Large Catechism may be read.

Lord's Prayer

Prayers for others and ourselves

Concluding prayer:
Lord Jesus, stay with us, for the evening is at hand and the day is past. Be our constant companion on the way, kindle our hearts, and awaken hope among us, that we may recognize You as You are revealed in the Scriptures and in the breaking of the bread. Grant this for Your name's sake. (444)
Amen.

Let us bless the Lord.   *[Psalm 103:1]*
Thanks be to God.

MEALTIME PRAYERS

Asking a Blessing

The children and members of the household shall go to the table reverently, fold their hands, and say:

The eyes of all look to You, [O Lord,] and You give them their food at the proper time. You open Your hand and satisfy the desires of every living thing. (Psalm 145:15–16)

Then shall be said the Lord's Prayer and the following:

Lord God, heavenly Father, bless us and these Your gifts which we receive from Your bountiful goodness, through Jesus Christ, our Lord. Amen.

Returning Thanks

Also, after eating, they shall, in like manner, reverently and with folded hands say:

Give thanks to the Lord, for He is good. His love endures forever. [He] gives food to every creature. He provides food for the cattle and for the young ravens when they call. His pleasure is not in the strength of the horse, nor His delight in the legs of a man; the Lord delights in those who fear Him, who put their hope in His unfailing love. (Psalm 136:1, 25; 147:9–11)

Then shall be said the Lord's Prayer and the following:

We thank You, Lord God, heavenly Father, for all Your benefits, through Jesus Christ, our Lord, who lives and reigns with You and the Holy Spirit forever and ever. Amen.

BEDTIME PRAYERS

Evening Prayer

In the evening when you go to bed, make the sign of the holy cross and say:

In the name of the Father and of the ☩ Son and of the Holy Spirit. Amen.

Then kneeling or standing, repeat the Creed and the Lord's Prayer. If you choose, you may also say this little prayer:

I thank You, my heavenly Father, through Jesus Christ, Your dear Son, that You have graciously kept me this day; and I pray that You would forgive me all my sins where I have done wrong, and graciously keep me this night. For into Your hands I commend myself, my body and soul, and all things. Let Your holy angel be with me, that the evil foe may have no power over me. Amen.

Then go to sleep at once and in good cheer.

THE APOSTLES' CREED

I believe in God, the Father Almighty,
    maker of heaven and earth.
And in Jesus Christ, His only Son, our Lord,
    who was conceived by the Holy Spirit,
    born of the virgin Mary,
    suffered under Pontius Pilate,
    was crucified, died and was buried.
    He descended into hell.
    The third day He rose again from the dead.
    He ascended into heaven
    and sits at the right hand of God the Father Almighty.
    From thence He will come to judge the living and the dead.
I believe in the Holy Spirit,
    the holy Christian Church,
        the communion of saints,
    the forgiveness of sins,
    the resurrection of the body,
    and the life everlasting. Amen.

THE LORD'S PRAYER

Our Father who art in heaven,

    hallowed be Thy name,

    Thy kingdom come,

    Thy will be done on earth as it is in heaven;

    give us this day our daily bread;

    and forgive us our trespasses as we forgive those

        who trespass against us;

    and lead us not into temptation,

    but deliver us from evil.

For Thine is the kingdom and the power and the glory

        forever and ever. Amen.

WORDS OF FAITH FOR FAMILIES

Below are several passages from Scripture for your use. Also included are the first stanzas of hymns about Baptism and hymns to sing in the morning and evening.

TEN COMMANDMENTS/LAW

And He said to him, "You shall love the Lord your God with all your heart and with all your soul and with all your mind. This is the great and first commandment. And a second is like it: You shall love your neighbor as yourself." (Matthew 22:37–39)

THE CREED

For God so loved the world, that He gave His only Son, that whoever believes in Him should not perish but have eternal life. (John 3:16)

PRAYER

Rejoice always, pray without ceasing, give thanks in all circumstances; for this is the will of God in Christ Jesus for you. (1 Thessalonians 5:16–18)

BAPTISM

For as many of you as were baptized into Christ have put on Christ. (Galatians 3:27)

CONFESSION AND ABSOLUTION

If we say we have no sin, we deceive ourselves, and the truth is not in us. If we confess our sins, He is faithful and just to forgive us our sins and to cleanse us from all unrighteousness. (1 John 1:8–9)

THE LORD'S SUPPER

The blood of Jesus His Son cleanses us from all sin. (1 John 1:7c)

LIFE AS A CHILD OF GOD

Hear, O Israel: The LORD our God, the LORD is one. You shall love the LORD your God with all your heart and with all your soul and with all your might. And these words that I command you today shall be on your heart. You shall teach them diligently to your children, and shall talk of them when you sit in your house, and when you walk by the way, and when you lie down, and when you rise. You shall bind them as a sign on your hand, and they shall be as frontlets between your eyes. You shall write them on the doorposts of your house and on your gates. (Deuteronomy 6:4–9)

But you are a chosen race, a royal priesthood, a holy nation, a people for His own possession, that you may proclaim the excellencies of Him who called you out of darkness into His marvelous light. (1 Peter 2:9)

Wives, submit to your husbands, as is fitting in the Lord. Husbands, love your wives, and do not be harsh with them. Children, obey your parents in everything, for this pleases the Lord. (Colossians 3:18–21)

Be kind to one another, tenderhearted, forgiving one another, as God in Christ forgave you. (Ephesians 4:32)

Children, obey your parents in the Lord, for this is right. "Honor your father and mother" (this is the first commandment with a promise), "that it may go well with you and that you may live long in the land." Fathers, do not provoke your children to anger, but bring them up in the discipline and instruction of the Lord. (Ephesians 6:1–4)

BAPTISMAL HYMNS

"BAPTIZED INTO YOUR NAME MOST HOLY"

Baptized into Your Name most holy,
O Father, Son, and Holy Ghost,
I claim a place, though weak and lowly,
Among Your saints, Your chosen host.
Buried with Christ and dead to sin,
Your Spirit now shall live within.

LSB 590:1

"SEE THIS WONDER IN THE MAKING"

See this wonder in the making:
God Himself this child is taking
As a lamb safe in His keeping,
His to be, awake or sleeping.

LSB 593:1

"GOD'S OWN CHILD, I GLADLY SAY IT"

God's own child, I gladly say it:
I am baptized into Christ!
He, because I could not pay it,
Gave my full redemption price.
Do I need earth's treasures many?
I have one worth more than any
That brought me salvation free
Lasting to eternity!

LSB 594:1

"ALL CHRISTIANS WHO HAVE BEEN BAPTIZED"

All Christians who have been baptized,
Who know the God of heaven,
And in whose daily life is prized
The name of Christ once given:
Consider now what God has done,
The gifts He gives to ev'ryone
Baptized into Christ Jesus!

LSB 596:1

MORNING HYMNS

"FATHER, WE PRAISE THEE"

Father, we praise Thee, now the night is over,
Active and watchful, stand we all before Thee;
Singing, we offer prayer and meditation:
Thus we adore Thee.

LSB 875:1

"WITH THE LORD BEGIN YOUR TASK"

With the Lord begin your task; Jesus will direct it.
For His aid and counsel ask; Jesus will perfect it.
Ev'ry morn with Jesus rise, And when day is ended,
In His name then close your eyes; Be to Him
    commended.

LSB 869:1

EVENING HYMNS

"EVENING AND MORNING"

Evening and morning, Sunset and dawning,
Wealth, peace and gladness, Comfort in sadness:
These are Thy works; all the glory be Thine!
Times without number, Awake or in slumber,
Thine eye observes us, From danger preserves us,
Causing Thy mercy upon us to shine.

LSB 726:1

"ALL PRAISE TO THEE, MY GOD, THIS NIGHT"

All praise to Thee, my God, this night
For all the blessings of the light.
Keep me, O keep me, King of kings,
Beneath Thine own almighty wings.

LSB 883:1